WELCOME TO THE WORLD OF MYSTERY SHOPPING

R. Lambert

Copyright © 2016 R. Lambert
All rights reserved.
ISBN: 1537513923
ISBN-13: 978-1537513928

CONTENTS

DISCLAIMER I
PREFACE III
1 IS MYSTERY SHOPPING FOR REAL? 1
2 WHAT IS MYSTERY SHOPPING? 3
3 WHY MYSTERY SHOP? 7
4 WOULD YOU MAKE A GOOD MYSTERY SHOPPER? 9
5 HOW TO BECOME A MYSTERY SHOPPER 11
6 HOW TO BECOME THE BEST MYSTERY SHOPPER WHO GETS THE BEST JOBS 15
7 HOW TO GET CERTIFIED 21
8 HOW TO DEAL WITH POTENTIAL ISSUES THAT CAN ARISE DURING A JOB 23
9 HOW TO GET PAID FOR REFERRALS 27
10 HOW TO FIND OTHER OPPORTUNITIES 29
11 RUNNING YOUR OWN BUSINESS 31
12 CONCLUSION 33
APPENDIX A – WHERE TO FIND MYSTERY SHOPPING COMPANIES 35
APPENDIX B – SAMPLE FORMS 39
REFERENCES 43

DISCLAIMER

Nothing in this book should be taken as legal or financial advice. This book is for informational purposes only. If you need legal or financial advice, please consult a qualified legal or financial advisor.

PREFACE

Have you ever gone into a restaurant, sat down at a dirty table, and waited forever for someone to greet you and take your order? Have you ever gone into a store and tried to find someone to help you, but couldn't? Have you ever gone into a business and seen things that needed to be repaired or employees who were playing around instead of helping customers? Have you ever gone into a retail store to purchase something, but had the employee who helped you adamantly steer you to look at a different brand, maybe something that was more expensive? Would you like to be able to do something about it? Would you like to do something about it that would help the business, make it more likely you'll have a better experience next time, and get paid for it at the same time?

If so, then you are in the right place! I am going to explain what mystery shopping is and how you can get paid to help businesses improve their customers' experiences. You can be a part of doing something fun and help the places you go get better all while getting paid.

1 IS MYSTERY SHOPPING FOR REAL?

Yes, mystery shopping is very real and tons of people get paid each year to do these jobs. According to the MSPA (Mystery Shopping Providers Association of North America), there are over 1,000,000 mystery shoppers. (FAQ, 2016) There are over 300 mystery shopping companies around the world. I have personally been doing mystery shopping for 10 years. I started when my daughter was four years old and even took her on shops with me. Though some companies will ask you not to take children because they can be distracting, my daughter was always very well behaved and even helped ask some of the questions we were instructed to ask. This made us seem like very natural, believable shoppers. She has grown up learning the business of being a mystery shopper and will be able to continue doing jobs herself.

I have also been an editor and trainer for a mystery shopping company for over four years. I love working as a mystery shopper and as an editor. It is so gratifying to know that I can have fun and make money while I am helping make so many different industries better.

2 WHAT IS MYSTERY SHOPPING?

Companies hire mystery shoppers to evaluate how well their employees are serving their customers and how effective their customer training programs are without the employees knowing they are being evaluated. It is a good way for employers to see what their employees would say and do with real customers, not just what they would do when the boss was around.

Mystery shopping has many names and is active in many different industries. Every company wants to know that their employees are carrying out the mission of the company and are treating customers in a way that will ensure they return to the business and maintain an on-going relationship. They want to know their employees are treating customers the way they have been trained to and in the way the owner of the business wants the customers to be treated. It is also a good way for businesses to check for areas that need improvement and to identify things being done that could put the business at risk or could prevent customers from coming back. It allows businesses to evaluate every aspect of the customer experience to see what they are doing well and what needs improvement.

In general terms, it involves accepting a job as an independent contractor to go into a business and do what you would normally do as a regular customer. You are playing a role, like an actor, but it is something you might normally do on any shopping trip or any night out to dinner. You must use good observation skills, pay attention to specific details or ask specific questions, and fill out a

WELCOME TO THE WORLD OF MYSTERY SHOPPING

report. Sometimes making observations includes keeping track of the time it takes for something to happen. Some jobs require a purchase and/or a return to be made.

Jobs can take 15 minutes up to about 8 hours. Most jobs take 30 minutes to 1 ½ hours on average. The time a job takes depends on the type of job, the number of tasks to be performed, whether driving to a location is involved, and the type of report required. Pay can range from $5 to $200, depending on the job. On average, mystery shopping pays $15-50 per job. You can always choose the types of assignments you want to do based on the time required and the pay. I typically choose jobs that pay an average of $10 to $15 per hour.

Since you are an independent contractor, you will need to pay taxes on what you earn and will need to carry your own insurance. We will discuss these items further in a future chapter.

What are some examples of mystery shop jobs?

- Going into a cell phone store to ask about new service and taking photos of the exterior

- Calling and visiting an apartment community as if you were looking for an apartment

- Visiting a retail electronics store and looking for several items to purchase and interacting with employees in those departments

- Making phone calls or visits to a business to verify their listing

WELCOME TO THE WORLD OF MYSTERY SHOPPING

details for a publication

- Checking merchandise, displays, and prices in a retail store

- Having dinner and/or a drink at a restaurant and making timed observations

- Going bowling and ordering a snack while there

- Visiting an amusement park and evaluating three beverage/food establishments while there

- Conducting revealed shops where you hand out awards to employees who successfully meet certain criteria

- Attending a large venue event and evaluating parking attendants and public facilities

- Standing outside a business and conducting brief surveys as customers exit

- Shopping at a retail store, interacting with one or more employees, making and purchase, and later returning the merchandise

- Getting an oil change

- Having service performed on your car or taking a test drive at a dealership

- Getting your taxes done and evaluating the person entering the data

- Going to a warehouse club and evaluating three

WELCOME TO THE WORLD OF MYSTERY SHOPPING

    demonstration/sample stands

- Visiting storage facilities and evaluating the customer service and the units

- Going to a bank and asking about information on getting a loan

The possibilities are vast and can lead to other assignments, like short-term demonstrations in established businesses for a particular product.

3 WHY MYSTERY SHOP?

There are several benefits to becoming a mystery shopper.

Flexibility

You can set your own hours to work, so you have flexibility in your schedule. This can help if you are a mother and need to work part-time, but want to be there to get your children on the bus in the morning and be there when they come home. It can also help if you are a student, but need to work a schedule around your classes.

It helped me as a single mom who worked a full-time job. I needed something I could do part-time during lunch, in the evenings, or on weekends that would not take me away from my daughter. I was able to do several jobs a week and still do everything else I had to do. I didn't have to pay a babysitter or take that time away from my daughter and I could work it around my schedule.

Pay

You can earn extra money being a mystery shopper. The amount you can earn is dependent only on your schedule, your willingness to follow the supplied guidelines for each job, and the number of companies you sign up with. With over 300 legitimate mystery shopping companies out there, you can sign up for as many as you want and only accept the assignments you want to do. You can even do shops while traveling to earn some extra money wherever you are. I have done jobs while taking a vacation or while visiting family in order to pay for the trip.

Related work

You also have the potential to be hired in a position that relates to mystery shopping. These positions can include scheduling, editing, auditing, in-store presentations, etc. Once you learn the ropes, you could even open your own mystery shopping company.

Referrals

Many companies will pay you for referrals of other mystery shoppers. They get the benefit of getting people who are usually good employees, since they are referred by people who already work for them. You get the benefit of helping your friends and family, and you get paid a small fee for each referral.

References

As a mystery shopper, you also gain valuable skills in the field of Customer Service. This can be a good reference for future employers. It can show them you are reliable, proactive, good with details and time management, and responsible. It also can show them you are willing to learn and worth an investment.

4 WOULD YOU MAKE A GOOD MYSTERY SHOPPER?

Be Reliable

A good mystery shopper on the most basic level is reliable. You have to read the documentation each company provides for the jobs you sign up for and you have to prepare for the assignment. If you say you can complete an assignment on a particular day, you need to be able to follow through and keep your word. Though things may happen once in a while, you should be consistent and should be someone the companies can rely on.

Follow the Instructions

Once you go out to conduct the shop, you need to follow the guidelines given. Be prepared to answer questions from consultants and sales people. Know the profile supplied for the shop and use that to answer questions. Know what you are supposed to ask and what you are not allowed to ask.

Be Observant

When you conduct a mystery shop, you must be very observant. You must be prepared to make observations as you arrive, during transitions or when moving from place-to-place, and at the end. You must be able to remember details, like the exact greeting and exact closing you are given by a consultant. You must be able to relay what happened and recall details room-by-room. You cannot summarize details, but must be specific about the facts.

You should not include opinion in any part of the report, except where you are specifically asked for an opinion. The companies want to know the facts. They will be able to gather from the details what happened.

Be Positive, Professional, and Give Good Selling Cues

During a shop, you must convey a positive attitude. Even if the consultant is being unkind or not doing their job, you are there to observe and report only. Do not respond in any way that would draw attention to yourself. Remain professional and neutral. Give the consultant good selling cues, meaning give them the impression that you are interested in what they are trying to sell. That gives them the opportunity to present a full sales presentation and ask for the sale. On most shops, except some retail shops, you will then be able to decline to complete the sale and tell them you will think about it.

5 HOW TO BECOME A MYSTERY SHOPPER

To become a mystery shopper, you have to find companies who are hiring independent consultants in your region. You should never pay for this information. When I was first starting out, I had heard of mystery shopping, but I couldn't find any way to get a list of the companies that hired mystery shoppers. The only thing I could find was a website offering membership that promised names of mystery shopping companies. The cost was less than $45 for a three-month membership. I took a chance and paid the money. I figured the only thing I would lose was the fee if it didn't work. Thankfully, they were legitimate and I was able to get the information and list of companies, and I started work right away. Now this information is more widely available. See the Appendix for a list of places where you can find current lists of legitimate mystery shopping companies.

After you find out who the companies are, you have to sign up at each of their websites. Signing up takes about 5-10 minutes for each website. They will ask for your name, address, phone number, email address, and your social security number. This is required, so they can send you payment. If you make over $600 with any of those companies in a year, they will send you a 1099 form for your taxes. Some companies pay by check and some pay by PayPal. Some companies pay you automatically, while others may require you to invoice them for the jobs you complete. Check with each company to see how they process payments.

Some companies will also ask what equipment you own

WELCOME TO THE WORLD OF MYSTERY SHOPPING

(digital phone, digital camera, audio recording equipment, video recording equipment, scanner, etc.) They may also ask about your likes. They are asking, because it helps them determine which type of shops you would be a good fit for.

As soon as you sign up, you can log into each site and begin finding jobs right away. Most of the websites will have a menu at the top. Most will have a heading similar to "Job Log," where you can find assignments in your area. You can go to that page and choose how near or far from your home zip code you want to search. If you are traveling, you can usually enter a zip code and search for that area as well.

In the list of search results, you can click on an item to see a description of the job. Some shops require you to meet with a "target" employee. Some jobs are "random," so you can meet with anyone at the business. If the shop involves a phone call and a visit, you will need to call the facility first using the provided profile and then meet with the same person onsite that you spoke with over the phone. Read over the description to see what the general requirements are for each job and follow the instructions to sign-up for the ones you are interested in.

You can sign up for multiple shops with multiple companies at the same time. It is important to keep a log or spreadsheet of each job you are assigned for each company. See the Appendix for a sample form you can use. It will give you the columns you can put into a spreadsheet program and adjust. Keep a record of the shop#, date due, business name/address/phone number, pay you are to receive, and any notes.

Be careful not to schedule too many shops during the same period or you can get overloaded. If you have to try several times to reach people by phone, it can also delay some shops and cause your due dates to overlap. It is best to start out with just a few shops spaced apart until you get your feet wet and you get a feel for what each job requires. Then you can begin assigning yourself more shops closer together once you know what to expect.

Each company will provide you with a manual, guidelines, instructions, or online training. Read through everything at first. After you have worked for a company for a while, you can then just concentrate on the profile for each shop and can scan through the instructions to see what may have changed.

Learn what to do for each shop in the event something doesn't go as planned. Know who to call and keep your scheduler's contact information with you in case you have to contact them during a shop.

Though it sounds like a lot, mostly it is reading what you are provided and paying attention to the details. Once you do a few shops, you will be experienced at it and it will only take a few minutes to prepare for a job.

6 HOW TO BECOME THE BEST MYSTERY SHOPPER WHO GETS THE BEST JOBS

- Remember this is a job. Do the work fully and according to the instructions.

- Prepare for each shop.

- Know what to do if something doesn't go as planned.

- Commit to a date and keep your commitments.

- If you make a mistake and forget to do something, be truthful. Most of the time you will still be paid. In some cases, you may receive partial payment, if the company has to have part of the shop redone by someone else. There may be times you won't get paid if you make a big mistake or cannot fulfil the requirements. This is very rare, as long as you follow the guidelines. I have only had 1 job not be paid in over 10 years and it was because I forgot to do a critical part of the shop.

- Always be polite and professional. Stay focused on the purpose. Do not waste the consultant's time with long conversations that are not relevant to the job you have been hired to do. I once had a shopper that extended the visit talking non-stop about their previous roommates and family. This was not relevant to the shop and took more time than it should have for the visit. Remember the employees you are evaluating have actual, paying customers to help. We are just supposed to get in, do the job, and get out. Allow them to do their job fully, but do not prolong the encounter.

- Check your work.

  - Make sure you have completed the forms completely.

  - Don't leave anything blank. Put "N/A" in any blanks that don't apply, so the company knows you did not accidently skip the question.

  - Review the information you have entered to make sure there are no answers that contradict.

  - If you have to write a narrative, make sure you have included ALL the details. Always include both sides of each conversation. Include each question you were asked and include your answer to each question. Include features and benefits you were told. Include conversations during transitions from place-to-place. You do not have to quote everything, but companies do want all the details. Consultants are being evaluated on how they sell and present. Reports will be returned to you if there is not enough detail.

  - Do not summarize! Be specific. Instead of saying someone "showed" you something, tell what they said about it or say how they showed it to you.

  - Leave out opinions, except in blanks where your opinions are asked for.

  - Write narratives, long answers, and short answers like a

story in paragraph format. Use complete sentences with proper spelling, grammar, and punctuation. Usually, companies want you to write in past tense, since what you are writing happened in the past. Check with each company on their standards.

- Make sure you indicate in your story each time the employee uses your name. This is important.

- Make sure to indicate each time the employee makes the effort to personalize the interaction. They can do this by telling personal stories or information about themselves or by asking about your work, likes, or family.

- Do not describe the consultant's ethnicity or weight unless the company specifically asks you to. Only describe them as male or female.

- Double check the dates and times you have listed to be sure they are correct.

- Submit your work on time. If you are going to be late, always let the scheduler know, so they can update their system. You will be seen as reliable if you keep the scheduler updated on the status of any shops you are assigned.

- If you are not sure about something, ask. Companies would much rather have you ask a question than have you go ahead and do something that causes them to have to do the shop over.

WELCOME TO THE WORLD OF MYSTERY SHOPPING

How to write the best mystery shopping report

- Use "apartment" or "home" instead of "unit" when talking about an apartment. When talking about a storage unit, the word "unit" is fine.

- Use "community" instead of "property."

- Use "consultant" rather than "agent."

- Use the consultant's name rather than writing "the employee" or "the leasing consultant" once you know what their name is. Make sure you spell their name the same way they do on their business card or on their name tag.

- Amenities in an apartment community include anything like a pool, tennis courts, playgrounds, hair salon, bus stop, etc.

- Features in an apartment community include things like the number of bedrooms, the number of bathrooms, ceiling fans, washers and dryers, appliances, walk-in closets, or patios/balconies.

- Benefits are anything that tells how the features would help you. For example, a consultant might tell you that having a washer and dryer in your apartment would keep you from having to go out to wash your laundry. They might tell you that having a fitness center would save you money on a gym membership.

- Focus more on the verbal interaction with the consultant than on the physical appearance of the store or community. Most companies will ask you about the front door, the welcome mat, the hours posted, or signs/advertisements. Notice these, but you do not need to describe the facility in detail. They are evaluating the consultant's selling skills, so this is the primary focus. Read over your shop report before completing your shop to see what questions they want you to answer. This will help you know what to focus on during your shop.

One way to ensure you are able to get all the details without forgetting things is to record the shops you do with a hand-held digital recorder. You can buy one online for about $40. It makes it much easier to write up your reports when you can go back and listen to the recording of your interaction and recall details the consultant told you that you might not have remembered otherwise.

You must check the regulations for the state where you live regarding recording before you record any interaction, though. Some states do not allow recording unless both parties are aware they are being recorded. Also, it is illegal to record any interaction in a financial institution or bank, so never record there. Check the laws in your state to make sure you know the laws before recording.

7 HOW TO GET CERTIFIED

There are two types of certification for mystery shopping: silver and gold. Certification is obtained through the MSPA. The silver certification training is online and gives you an introductory look at mystery shopping and the basic skills needed to conduct shops. The cost is $15 as of the time of this printing.

The gold certification costs $75. The training can be taken in a classroom setting or online. See the following links:

MSPA Silver Certification –

http://www.mspanorthamerica.com/shoppers/silver2.php?trk=profile_certification_title

MSPA Gold Certification –

http://www.mspa-na.org/certification#intro

There is also training available through the MSPA for Industry Writing and Video Shopping.

For most shoppers, getting silver certified online is sufficient. You have to weigh for yourself if paying the fee for getting gold certified is worth it for you. From my years in mystery shopping, I did not see where the gold certification generated an increase in pay. I also saw very few shoppers who were gold certified.

8 HOW TO DEAL WITH POTENTIAL ISSUES THAT CAN ARISE DURING A JOB

The first thing to remember is that you are playing a part you were hired to play and are following a profile. If something unexpected happens, like the consultant does not show up for your appointment or they pass you off to another employee instead of helping you, don't panic. You can excuse yourself and say you just got a text or you can say you left something in your car. Go outside and call or text the scheduler for your shop and ask them what they want you to do. They will know what the client allows in these circumstances and will let you know how to handle the situation. Sometimes, they will have you return at a later date or time. Sometimes, they will have you proceed to complete the shop with the employee you were handed off to. If you are not sure, always ask. It is better to ask what to do up front than it is to proceed based on your own assumptions and have the shop be rejected.

If a shop is rejected for not following directions or for lack of detail in the report, no one on the mystery shopping team gets paid – not you, the shopper; not the scheduler; not the editor; and not the owner. This is not a common occurrence, but it does happen. If you do your best to prepare and read the instructions and the profile ahead of time, if you keep good notes, if you fill in all the details without leaving holes or gaps in your story, and if you submit your report by the deadline, everything should be fine. There are a lot of shoppers out there who are trying to do just enough to get by. This is not what mystery shopping companies are looking for. They invest time and training into shoppers in order to get quality reports for their clients. Don't be one of those shoppers. Be one who invests themselves into learning the rules and doing quality work. Do what you say you will do on time. You will get a lot more out of it and have more fun doing it if you do.

The shops I have seen that were rejected were ones where the shoppers did not do those things. They did not read the instructions. They tried to rush through writing up the details and had a lot of missing information. They did not complete their shops or did not follow the instructions. They did not meet deadlines or did not respond to the mystery shopping company when they were contacted for questions. Those are the things that will cause a shop not to be paid. Those are also things that will cause you to receive a citation.

Citations are notes schedulers and editors keep on shoppers behind the scenes. If a shopper does a great job and goes above and beyond in their shop and report, they can receive a "Hero" citation. They will be the first to be assigned jobs in the future.

If a shopper does not do what they were asked, misses deadlines, or consistently makes the same mistakes over and over, they can receive a negative citation. These are given by number and have a weight. If you did a poor job on a report and did not respond when they asked you to fix it or if you "flaked" on the job and did not complete it after it was assigned, you could receive a number like a 5 out of 10. They would give that a "weight," the number of jobs this grade would apply to. When assigning jobs to those who have applied for them in the future, the mystery shopping scheduler will take these citations into account before assigning you more work. They need reliable, quality shoppers and will give the jobs to those shoppers who prove themselves.

You have to think about this as a job. Though it is fun and very flexible, you do have to treat it just as you would any other job where you want to get paid. As an employee of a company, if you do not follow the rules or you do not complete your assignments in a timely manner with quality work, you probably will not be an employee at that company for very long. At the very least, you would not get promotions or raises.

Do quality work and have fun. You can enjoy this work for the rest of your life and can be one of those who gets high grades and gets called for special assignments again and again.

9 HOW TO GET PAID FOR REFERRALS

Some companies will pay you for referring other shoppers to them. If you do a good job as a mystery shopper or auditor, then the companies you work for will trust you to bring them others like you who will do a good job. They know this will benefit them and they will often pay you a fee for referring others. It is in your best interest to refer people who will have a similar work ethic to yours and who will do quality work on a consistent basis. Check each company's website for details on how to refer others and on the fee they offer for referrals

10 HOW TO FIND OTHER OPPORTUNITIES

Once you have some experience working for different companies completing shops, you can often get hired as a consultant to do more consistent work. For instance, if a mystery shopping company likes the way you write up your reports with good spelling and grammar and good details, they may invite you to work for them as an editor. You would have more consistent work and a steadier income, while still having flexibility in your schedule. As an editor, you would edit the reports submitted by other shoppers. You would be checking to be sure all the details are there and correcting spelling, grammar, and formatting before submitting to the client.

The companies might also invite you to work with them as a scheduler. As a scheduler, you would setup the shops requested by the clients and would choose shoppers from those who apply to do each shop. You would be responsible for keeping a list of all outstanding jobs and checking in with shoppers to see how their shops are progressing. You would be responsible for updating the owner and clients on the progress and of any issues.

You could also be offered steady work for clients doing sales presentations inside retail stores or you could become a regular auditor for a particular company. There are many options available once you find your way into the field of mystery shopping and auditing. And one of the best parts is that you get to choose how much or how little to work.

11 RUNNING YOUR OWN BUSINESS

There are many books out there on running your own business, so I will just cover the basics here as they apply to mystery shopping. As a mystery shopper or auditor, you are an independent contractor. That means you are self-employed. Setting up a business is fairly simple, but you need to check the city, county, and federal regulations for your area to see what the requirements are for your location.

Typically, you will need to come up with a business name and register it with the city or county. This is currently about $15. You will need to make sure the name you choose is not already registered in your location. You will need to determine the regulations for a Tax ID number or EIN. Some locations allow you to use your social security number. Others may require you to have a separate Tax ID number or EIN for your business. In addition, you may need to report any assets you use in your business, such as a computer or sometimes your car.

As mentioned above, you will need a system to keep track of each job you do for each company. You will also want to keep a record of any mileage you have for each job or other expenses. It is a good idea to keep copies of all documents supplied for each shop to store with each year's taxes for the required time period. I usually just jot down my mileage right on the back of the supporting documents, so I have everything for that job all together in one place. There may be other tax forms you would need to file when you file your state and federal taxes, so check on those as well.

As stated before, this should not be taken as legal or financial advice. I am just trying to help you think of things you need to plan for or check on as part of being self-employed. Often, people forget this is a business, so they overlook things they need to do to setup a business or to pay taxes.

12 CONCLUSION

Hopefully, I have given you a glimpse into the world of mystery shopping and have answered most of your questions about this field. To me, it is a great opportunity to have a fun job with a flexible schedule and good pay. It is rewarding to know you are helping businesses improve their customer service and you are building your own business in the process. I have always had fun with it and I hope you do too.

Take a look at the resources at the end of the book, where you will find lists of mystery shopping companies at no additional charge to you. You will also find a sample spreadsheet for keeping up with the jobs you complete. Happy shopping!

APPENDIX A – WHERE TO FIND MYSTERY SHOPPING COMPANIES

List 1: MSPA Member Companies:

http://www.mspanorthamerica.com/shoppers/membercos.php

List 2:

http://www.quirks.com/directory/shopping/

List 3 (Just search for their name and the word "shopper"):

- Amber Arch Ltd
- Ann Michaels & Associates
- AQ Services
- ath Power Consulting Corporation
- BARE International
- Beyond Hello
- Caliber
- Cirrus Marketing Consultants
- Compliance Solutions Worldwide
- Confero Inc.
- Consumer Service Analysis LLC

WELCOME TO THE WORLD OF MYSTERY SHOPPING

- Corporate Risk Solutions
- Customer Experience Experts
- Customer Impact
- Customer Service Experts
- Data Quest Ltd.
- DJC
- GfK
- HDE
- Insight Market Research
- Intellishop
- KSS Intl Inc.
- LG Market Research
- Market Viewpoint
- Marketing Endeavors
- Mercantile Systems & Surveys
- Mystery Shoppers Inc.
- PAN Research Ltd.
- Phantom Shoppers

WELCOME TO THE WORLD OF MYSTERY SHOPPING

- Pinnacle
- Reality Based Group
- Remington Evaluations
- Research Services Group
- Service Impressions
- Service Performance Group, Inc.
- Service Savvy
- Service Sleuth
- ServiceCheck.com
- Shoppers Inc.
- Shoppers' View
- Technology Store Shopper
- The Retail Outsource

APPENDIX B – SAMPLE FORMS

Sample Job Spreadsheet

Shop#	Community Name	Company	Pay for This Job	Type of Job	Notes	Invoice#	Invoice Date	Date Paid

WELCOME TO THE WORLD OF MYSTERY SHOPPING

Sample Invoice

SHOPPER INVOICE

Shopper Name

INVOICE # [   ]
DATE: OCTOBER 30, 2016

Street Address
City, State ZIP

Phone
Email:
Shopper ID#

WELCOME TO THE WORLD OF MYSTERY SHOPPING

To Mystery Shopper Company
Name
Address

SHOP# - DATE SHOPPED	COMPANY SHOPPED, CONSULTANT SHOPPED	LOCATION	PAY DUE
	Total		

REFERENCES

FAQ. (2016, 09 04). Retrieved from MSPA North America: http://www.mspa-na.org/faq

www.ingramcontent.com/pod-product-compliance
Lightning Source LLC
Chambersburg PA
CBHW070412190526
45169CB00003B/1231